BUILDING KITCHEN CABINETS MANUAL

THE ART OF BUILDING KITCHEN CABINETS SIMPLIFIED

CHARLIE PONDS

Table of Contents

CHAPTER ONE

The Art of Building Kitchen Cabinets

If you want to save money on your next renovation, learning how to build your own cabinets is a great place to start.

Putting together custom cabinetry for your kitchen, bathroom, or built-ins is easier than you might think. Simple boxes are all that separate most cabinets from the ground. When the cabinets are set up, the seams won't be visible from the outside either.

I built all the cabinets for our do-it-yourself kitchen remodel last year. I avoided spending a ton of money by building sturdy cabinets from scratch. How I built my cabinets and the cheap tools I used are detailed here.

And so, if you're interested in learning how to construct cabinets for your own renovations, I'll explain everything step by step.

If you're going to do cabinets, it's best to do them yourself.

In comparison to buying pre-fabricated cabinets or spending a fortune on custom cabinets, building your own offers many advantages.

I. You'll have a significant financial benefit! Building your own cabinets can save you thousands of dollars compared to purchasing pre-fab or custom cabinets, and even just one or two tools will do the trick.

Second, there are no visible gaps. Unlike prefabricated cabinets, which typically come in 3-inch increments and leave gaps that need to be filled with spacers, custom-built cabinets can be made to any size.

Thirdly, a fully personalized kitchen is within your reach. Need a set of drawers at the bottom? Taller than average base cupboards? Extensions in the vertical? Your custom cabinetry can be made to accommodate any imaginable item.

You will experience a sensation that is simply incredible. The fact that you constructed your own cupboards will astound and amaze visitors. And when you're done, you'll feel like nothing can stop you.

CHAPTER TWO

Cabinetry Varieties

The two most common types of cabinets on the market and in new construction are face frame cabinets and frameless cabinets (or Euro-style cabinets). You can construct either of these types of cabinets.

It all depends on your preferred aesthetic for deciding which one to use. In every case, pros and cons can be found. Make your decision based on personal taste and the overall look you wish to achieve in the room.

Just what is a face frame cabinet?

Cabinets with a frame across the front of the cabinet box are known as face frame cabinets. Plywood is used to create the box, with a solid wood face frame (1x2s are commonly used) attached to the front to conceal the plywood edge. When we remodeled our kitchen, we stuck with what we considered to be the most American of cabinet styles: face frame cabinets.

Aside from the usual rails and stiles, additional rails are used to create the face frames around doors and drawers. If the face frame is in the way, you'll either need to use special slides for face frames or add blocking to the sides of the drawer to make it level with the face frame.

Doors for cabinets can be either overlay (mounted directly onto the face frame) or inset (mounted inside the cabinet carcass) (they sit inside the face frame and are flush with the front). Depending on the type of hinges you go with, overlay cabinet doors can have a large reveal of the face frame or a small reveal for a more contemporary look.

The Value of a Face Frame Cabinet

Hinge sets for overlay doors on face frame cabinets are readily available in the United States.

• Alignment of cabinet doors is not critical for their attractiveness (the face frame offers some wiggle room).

The cabinet box can be constructed using pre-finished plywood, reducing the amount of finishing work to just the thin face frame.

With a 1/4" tolerance on the face frame's edge, installing the cabinets may be simpler.

Excellent for repairing crooked walls (which they all are).

An explanation of the term "frameless cabinet" would be appreciated.

A plywood only cabinet is called a frameless cabinet because there is no supporting frame. Edge banding is used to complete the exposed plywood edges. It was Ikea that popularized what are sometimes called "European style" cabinets.

This cabinet layout is very minimalist and contemporary.

Keeping the cabinet box square is a challenge when working with frameless cabinets. Assembling a straight line of cabinets and hanging doors with a flush reveal can be difficult if the wall is not square.

Both overlay and inset door styles can be used for a frameless cabinet. For frameless cabinets, the only overlay choice is a full overlay, which completely conceals the cabinet frames (to within about an eighth of an inch).

CHAPTER THREE

What a Frameless Cabinet Can Do For You

• The front of the cabinet lacks a frame, so there is no lip around the edge against which you can bang things while loading or unloading.

Because you don't have to use solid wood for the face frame, they're also less expensive to produce.

• There is no need to construct and finish the face frame after the box is complete; it can be installed immediately.

Methods for Constructing a Cupboard

Given the wide variety of possible cabinet boxes, this post will serve as a high-level introduction to the process of constructing cabinets. I'll do my best to go into detail about all the different kinds of cabinets. If there is something you want to know about this topic that I did not cover, please leave a comment below.

What you'll need (here's a comprehensive list of the cheap tools I used to build my cabinets):

• A sawing device such as a circular saw or table saw fitted with guides

• I rely heavily on my circular saw equipped with the Kreg Accucut and Ripcut because I lack the table saw skills necessary to cut down a full sheet of 3/4" plywood by myself. You can get the job done with just these two items if you take your time and measure carefully at every stage. With a table saw, you only have to adjust the fence once to make cuts of uniform length.

Hardware: • Jig for making pocket holes

Pocket holes are faster, easier, and stronger than the conventional method of building cabinet boxes with rabbets and dados. Further, the pocket holes are concealed, so no one will know you took the quick route.

Check out this list of the top rated Kreg pocket hole jigs to see which one is right for you.

Cutoff saw

When cutting face frames, I find that the miter saw is the most accurate and efficient tool to use. For frameless cupboards, this is unnecessary.

A Drill and an Impact Driver

• A tape measure

• Squares

- Clamps

Equipment: Shop vacuum, optional

Subcomponents of a Storage Cabinet

First, let's inspect the cabinet box's constituent parts. There are some subtle distinctions between these components for a face frame cabinet and a frameless cabinet.

Cabinet carcasses will have two sides made from 3/4" plywood. Building kitchen cabinets requires uniformity of size between the base and wall cabinets. The cabinets above the refrigerator and the pantry can be extended if necessary.

To keep the box square and sturdy, you can either use 3/4-inch plywood for the back of the cabinet or support it with 3-4-inch pieces of 3/4-inch plywood. Then, you can cover the back with 1/4-inch plywood. Particularly useful for cabinets that require access holes for plumbing. Using 1/4" plywood for the back of a large cabinet project is another great way to save money.

In a cabinet, "bottom" refers to the very bottom shelf. It should be flush with the top of the toe-kick of the base cabinets. It has no lip because it rests flush with the top of the bottom face frame rail in wall cabinets that use a face frame.

A toe-kick is a small extension of the base cabinet that sits above the floor. The cabinet side can be trimmed to accommodate the toe-kick. Alternatively, you can construct a 24 box on the floor to serve as the toe-kick for larger sections of cabinets. When working with large spans of cabinets, this is helpful because more sides can be cut from a 4' x 8' sheet of plywood if the standard cabinet height is used. Moreover, the 24 box can be easily leveled before the cabinets are installed.

In general, a countertop replaces the top of a base cabinet, so such cabinets do not include a top piece. The cabinet box is kept square and secure with supports, and the cabinet is finished off with the installation of the counters. You can use a top in place of a countertop when constructing built-ins.

Smaller pieces of plywood (typically 3–4 inches wide and the width of the cabinet carcass) called "supports" are used to maintain the cabinet box's squareness and stability. If your cabinet has a countertop, you can skip using the top piece and use either 1 or 2. If your cabinets don't have frames, you'll need to use something to hold the drawers apart.

Cabinets with a face frame are distinguished by a separate front frame that is attached to the carcass. Stiles (the vertical part of the face frame that runs the full height of the cabinet) and rails (the horizontal part that runs the width of the face) make up the face frame (running horizontally between the stiles).

CHAPTER FOUR

Making the Cabinet's Bones

The box's plywood carcass serves as the cabinet's framework. This is the full construction process for frameless cabinets. The face frame of your cabinets goes up next, and then the two halves are joined together.

Perfecting Your Cabinet Boxes: Advice

Perfect cabinet boxes can be made if all of the parts are

square and the angles are cut to 90 degrees. Then the only difficulty in installation will be adjusting to the uneven walls.

Make sure the blade is at a perfect 90 degrees to the tool's bed or plate before beginning any woodcutting. If you're off by just one degree, your boxes and picture frames won't be square.

Second, you can't just cut everything to size. When you cut plywood, the blade will remove a tiny bit of material, called a kerf, from the board (resulting in non-square cabinet boxes). Instead, take the necessary measurements and make the first cut. After that, you can take your measurements from the fresh edge to the subsequent cut line. Make sure the blade's edge is on the outside of the cut line, allowing you to discard the entire measured quantity.

Measure from the top right corner across to the bottom left corner to quickly check if all pieces you cut are square. Take note of the scale. Then, gauge the distance between the four corners. A square shape is indicated by measurements that are all the same.

#1 - Segment the Plywood

When building a large number of cabinets, it is important to plan out how you will cut the pieces from the plywood sheets in advance. Plywood side pieces should have their grain running vertically. The grain should run from side to side rather than from front to back in horizontal pieces.

Plywood can be easily cut with a circular saw and guide track if you lay a 2" thick piece of rigid foam on the ground or your work table and then set the plywood on top of that.

If the plywood isn't square, cut the shorter side to make it so that it's the same length as the longer one. When you're ready, go ahead and cut everything out. To facilitate assembly later, label the pieces as you go.

Cut the support pieces from scraps of plywood left over from larger cuts.

Tip #2: Create Pocket Holes

To make holes in material up to three quarters of an inch thick, adjust your pocket hole jig's settings accordingly. The Kreg Jig K4 system is fantastic, and I use it for the vast majority of my woodworking endeavours.

The bottom, top, and support pieces should all have pocket

holes drilled on both sides. The number of pocket holes you need to drill is proportional to the length of your piece. At the very least, every four to five inches is ideal. Remember to put two of the end pieces in each end for support.

When building cabinets with a face frame, it's necessary to make pocket holes in the front of the base, ceiling, and walls before you can attach the face frame. Remember that drilling the pocket holes before putting everything together will make things much simpler.

Toe-kicks on base cabinets should be removed at this time. The toe kick is usually between 4 and 2 1/2 inches high and 2 to 3 inches deep, but can be trimmed to fit with ease using a jigsaw.

Step Three: Put Together the Box

Wood glue should be used on all the joints to ensure the longevity of your cabinet box. In the case of pre-finished plywood, regular wood glue will not adhere properly. Melamine glue should be used instead (I love this RooClear Glue).

The exterior (the side with the pocket holes) should be facing down as you lay one of the side pieces on your work surface. Clamp the bottom piece to the side piece after applying glue to the side.

Keep the bottom of the base cabinet flush with the toe-kick or the floor (if no toe-kick). Set the top of the bottom piece 1 1/2 inches up from the bottom to ensure it is flush with the top of the bottom face frame rail when installing wall cabinets. (12 face frame is 1 1/2 inches tall.

The same method should be used to fasten the top piece (or support, if none is required) in place. The top will meet the top of the side pieces at a perfect 90 degree angle. The supports must meet the front of the side pieces at a flush level.

The pieces that go between the drawers should be attached as support for the frameless cabinets.

Apply glue and pocket hole screws to permanently attach the back piece (if using 3/4" plywood) or another support so that the top is flush with the back.

The last step is to join the opposite end. Put the bottom, top, and support pieces in place with glue, and make sure they are aligned. Make sure everything is square before clamping it all together, and then fasten it with pocket hole screws.

Backing can be made from 1/4" plywood by measuring and cutting to size. As mentioned in the advice section, double check that the box is square before proceeding with attaching the plywood back with glue and brad nails.

Use a scrap of 1/4" plywood to complete the toe-kick. If you'd like, you can use thicker plywood; just be sure to adjust the toe-dimensions kick's accordingly.

Creating a Skeleton for the Face

Trim the stiles and rails to size.

Unless your cabinets have a toe-kick, the stiles will be at the same height as the carcass. The top of the bottom shelf in toe-kick cabinets should be level with the top of the face frame rail. If your plywood is 3/4 inches thick and your face frame is 1x2s (1 1/2 inches thick), then the stiles should be 3/4 inches longer than the side length minus the toe-kick.

2.The width of the rails will be the width of the cabinet minus the width of the face frame (x2) plus 1/2 inches. The extra half inch will cause the face frame to protrude past the side of the cabinet box by 1/4 inch, allowing for more flexibility during installation.

Each cabinet will typically consist of two rails and four stiles. Each drawer should have a rail installed at its base. When installing doors on large cabinets, a center stile can help.

Make sure the rail pieces have two pocket holes drilled into each edge (and center stile if you have those). Wood glue the rail end flush with the top of the stile and set it in place. Clamp the pieces together with a face clamp to ensure that the flat surfaces of both pieces are maintained during assembly. Fasten using pocket hole screws that are 1 1/4 inches in length.

It's worth mentioning that you should do the same thing with the opposite rail at the stile's base.

The second stile is attached to the end of the rails using wood glue.

If you want to add a center rail, find the exact middle and secure it now.

CHAPTER FIVE

Putting the Final Touches on the Cabinets

For cabinets with a face frame:

You can now attach the face frame to the cabinet box if you intend to paint, stain, or seal the two to look like one cohesive unit. You should start by painting, staining, or sealing the face frame and the sides if you used pre-finished plywood.

Learn the steps to painting raw cabinetry right here.

Wood glue should be applied to the plywood cabinet carcass's edge before the face frame is attached. Since the face frame's plywood sides and back are left unfinished, no melamine glue is required.

Make sure the face frame is clamped to the cabinet box squarely, and that it extends past the edge by at least 1/4 inch. Fasten the face frame in place with 1 1/4-inch pocket hole screws in the pre-drilled holes.

It is finally time to put up those cabinets you built yourself!